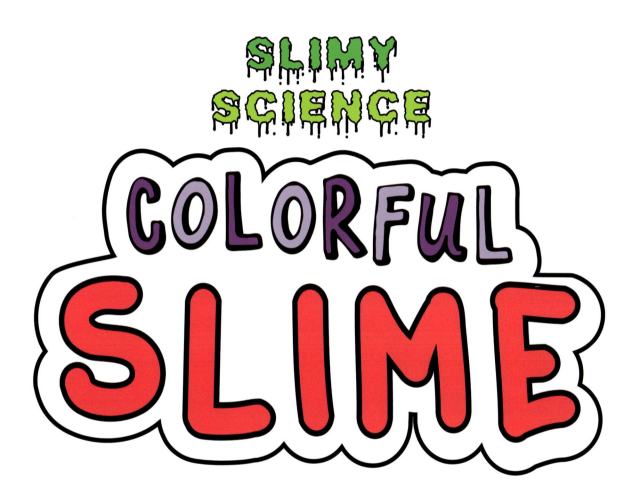

BY
LOUISE NELSON

Published in 2022 by Windmill Books,
an Imprint of Rosen Publishing
29 East 21st Street, New York, NY 10010

© 2022 Booklife Publishing
This edition is published by arrangement with Booklife Publishing

All rights reserved. No part of this book may be reproduced in any form without permission in writing from the publisher, except by a reviewer.

Edited by: Madeline Tyler
Illustrated by: Danielle Rippengill

Cataloging-in-Publication Data

Names: Nelson, Louise.
Title: Colorful slime / Louise Nelson.
Description: New York : Windmill, 2022. | Series: Slimy science | Includes glossary and index.
Identifiers: ISBN 9781499489453 (pbk.) | ISBN 9781499489477 (library bound) | ISBN 9781499489460 (6pack) | ISBN 9781499489484 (ebook)
Subjects: LCSH: Gums and resins, Synthetic--Juvenile literature. | Handicraft--Juvenile literature.
Classification: LCC TP978.N45 2022 | DDC 620.1'924--dc23

Printed in the United States of America

CPSIA Compliance Information: Batch CWWM22: For Further Information contact Rosen Publishing, New York, New York at 1-800-237-9932

SAFETY AND RESPONSIBILITY INFO FOR GROWN-UPS

Any ingredients used could cause irritation, so don't play with slime for too long, don't put it near your face, and keep it away from babies and young children.

Always wash your hands before and after making slime. Choose kid-safe glues and non-toxic ingredients, and always make sure there is an adult present.

Don't substitute ingredients—we cannot guarantee the results.

Leftover slime can be stored for one more use for up to a week in a sealed container and out of the reach of children. For hygiene reasons, we do not recommend storing slime that has been used in a classroom environment.

Slime is not safe for pets.

Wear a mask around powdered ingredients and goggles around liquid ingredients. Before throwing your slime away, cut it into lots of small pieces. Don't put slime down the drain—always put it in the trash.

COLORED SLIME!

IMAGE CREDITS: All images are courtesy of Shutterstock.com, unless otherwise specified. With thanks to Getty Images, Thinkstock Photo and iStockphoto. Cover – Zhe Vasylieva, balabolka, Dado Photos, xnova, Lithiumphoto, New Africa, Natallia Boroda. Images used on every page: Heading Font – Zhe Vasylieva. Background – Lithiumphoto. Grid – xnova. Splats – Sonechko57. 2 – MonicaJohansen. 4 – jarabee123. 5 – Kabardins photo, Efetova Anna, 6 – Rosalie Kreulen. 7 – New Africa. 8 – Stenko Vlad, VLADIMIR VK. 10 – P Maxwell Photography, Sylwia Brataniec. 11 – Natallia Boroda. 14 – Stenko Vlad, VLADIMIR VK. 17 – Vacharapong W. 18 – Ory Gonian, AlonaPhoto, andras_csontos. 19 – Efetova Anna, Ory Gonian, AlesiaKan. 20 – Mihael Mihalev. 21 – nikamo. 22 – loocmill, Olga Stabredov, Hong Vo. 23 – Efetova Anna, Anna Aibetova, MonicaJohansen.

CONTENTS

PAGE 4   IT'S SLIME TIME!
PAGE 6   THE SCIENCE OF SLIME
PAGE 8   PRIMARY SLIME
PAGE 9   SAFETY FIRST!
PAGE 10   TIME FOR SLIME
PAGE 12   SECONDARY SCHOOL
PAGE 14   MAKING PREDICTIONS
PAGE 16   MIX IT UP!
PAGE 18   BLACK AND WHITE
PAGE 19   ALL THAT GLITTERS
PAGE 20   COMPLEMENTARY COLORS
PAGE 22   PASTELS AND NEONS
PAGE 24   GLOSSARY AND INDEX

Words that look like this can be found in the glossary on page 24.

IT'S SLIME TIME!

Slime. It's bouncy, stretchy, oozy fun—but do you know what it is? It's not quite liquid and not quite solid . . . so what is it?

!! NERD ALERT !!
Slime is a non-Newtonian fluid. This means that it doesn't act like other liquids, such as water or milk.

The everyday objects we use are all made from different materials. Materials can be natural or human-made. They are good for different jobs because of their different properties.

SLIME IS A MATERIAL THAT HAS THE FOLLOWING PROPERTIES:

- NOT QUITE SOLID
- MOLDABLE
- STRETCHY
- FLOWS BUT NOT RUNNY
- NOT QUITE LIQUID

THE SCIENCE OF SLIME

Many animals make their own natural slime. Tree frogs have a sticky slime on their feet that helps them stick to trees. This slime is called mucus.

!! NERD ALERT !!
Scientists have studied this mucus and hope to copy it. Maybe one day we could all have non-slip shoes!

WE CAN ALSO MAKE SLIME WITH SCIENCE!

Never touch chemicals without an adult!

When we mix two chemicals together, it can change their properties. By mixing the correct chemicals together, we can turn liquids, powders, and other things into slime!

PRIMARY SLIME

!! NERD ALERT !!
You can make other colors by mixing the primary colors together. Find out more on page 12!

Red, yellow, and blue are primary colors. You can't make the primary colors by mixing any other colors together.

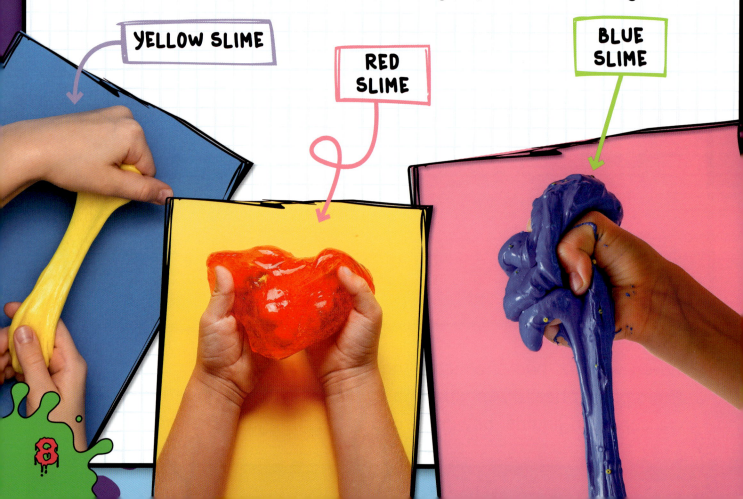

YELLOW SLIME

RED SLIME

BLUE SLIME

SAFETY FIRST!

THE GOLDEN RULES

1. Always make slime with a grown-up.

2. Don't swap in other ingredients because different <u>reactions</u> could happen.

3. DON'T EAT SLIME, and keep it away from your face.

!! NERD ALERT !!
If you are <u>sensitive</u> to any ingredients, wear long sleeves and gloves or use a different recipe.

TIME FOR SLIME

LET'S MAKE SOME SLIME IN THE PRIMARY COLORS. YOU WILL NEED:

- [ ] 4 ounces (about 100 ml) of white or clear school glue (PVA)
- [ ] Half a tablespoon of baking soda
- [ ] 1 teaspoon of contact lens solution
- [ ] Gel or powder food coloring in the primary colors
- [ ] Safety first!

DON'T FORGET!
Always make slime with a responsible adult!

FOOD COLORING

Always make slime with a grown-up, and wear gloves and an apron while mixing.

METHOD:

1. Add the baking soda and glue into a bowl. Mix well.

2. Add the contact lens solution and a few drops of color, and mix.

3. The slime will begin to form. It will look stringy at first so keep mixing!

4. After about 30 seconds, the slime will come together.

Make three batches of slime, one in each primary color.

SECONDARY SCHOOL

When you mix two primary colors together, you make a secondary color. Orange, purple, and green are all secondary colors.

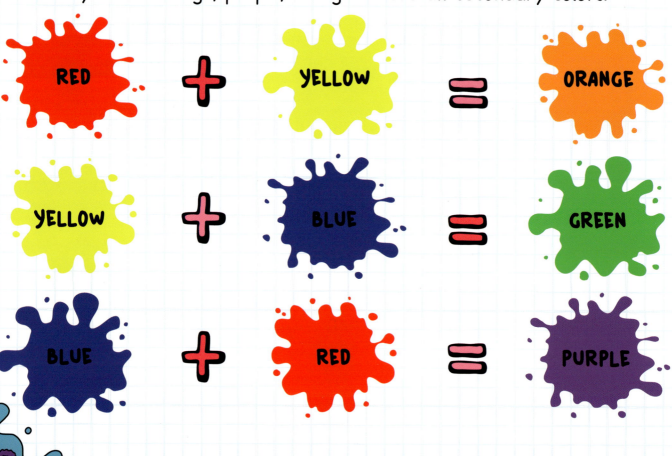

We can see how the colors mix by looking at a color wheel. Can you point to the secondary colors? They sit between the two colors that are mixed to make them.

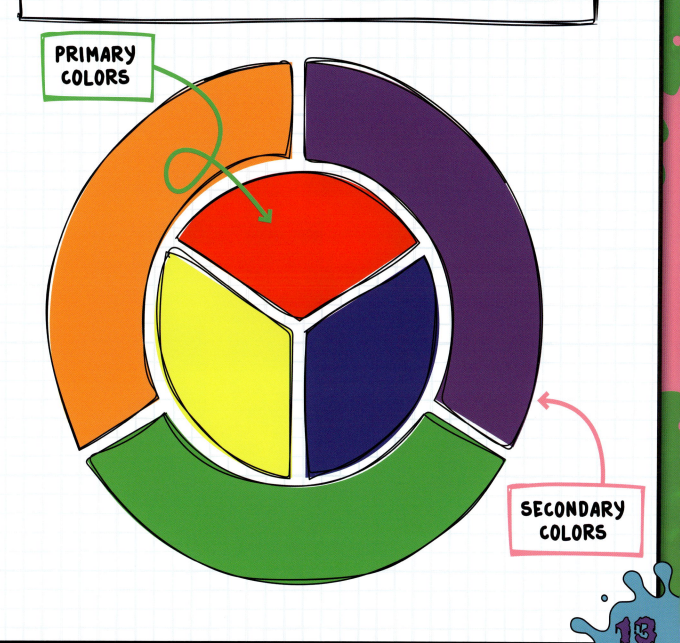

PRIMARY COLORS

SECONDARY COLORS

MAKING PREDICTIONS

When scientists want to do an experiment, they first make a prediction. This means they work out what they think is going to happen. We are going to mix two primary colors together by using slimes in different colors. What do we predict will happen?

Scientists can use what they already know to make a prediction. This diagram shows what happens when we mix two primary colors. We can use it to predict what will happen with our slime.

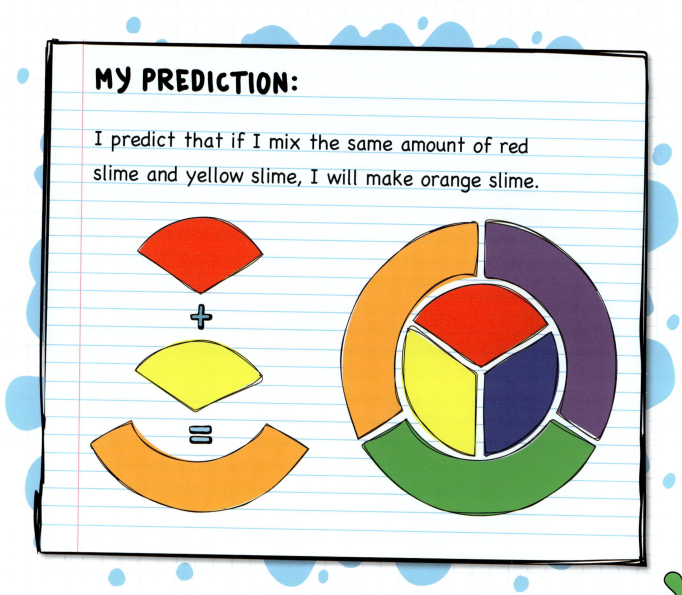

MY PREDICTION:

I predict that if I mix the same amount of red slime and yellow slime, I will make orange slime.

MIX IT UP!

PREDICT WHAT WILL HAPPEN WHEN YOU MIX TWO DIFFERENT COLORS OF SLIME!

1. Take two bits of slime, both in different primary colors.

2. Tear off small pieces of your primary-colored slime.

3. Mix and mash your slimes together.

4. Squish and smush them until they are completely mixed.

!! NERD ALERT !!
Remember to use the same amount of each color.

NOW LOOK AT YOUR PREDICTION.

Were you correct? Did you get any unexpected results?

Can you make a slime rainbow? These slimes have been swirled together.

What happens if you mix a little of all the colors together?

BLACK AND WHITE

Make a batch of slime using the recipe, but don't add any color. Then make another, and add black food coloring to the slime. Mixing small amounts of these together creates different shades of gray.

!! NERD ALERT !!
Black, white, and gray are neutral colors.

BLACK SLIME

WHITE SLIME

GRAY SLIME

ALL THAT GLITTERS

Gold and silver slimes

Very *fine* glitter makes awesome metallic slime.

What color glitter will you use?

Mix glitter into your slime to get interesting results! The more glitter you add, the more metallic and shiny your slime will be! Gold, silver, and copper are metallic colors.

COMPLEMENTARY COLORS

Complementary colors are pairs of colors that are opposite each other on the color wheel.

!! NERD ALERT !!
Each pair of complementary colors is made up of one primary color and one secondary color.

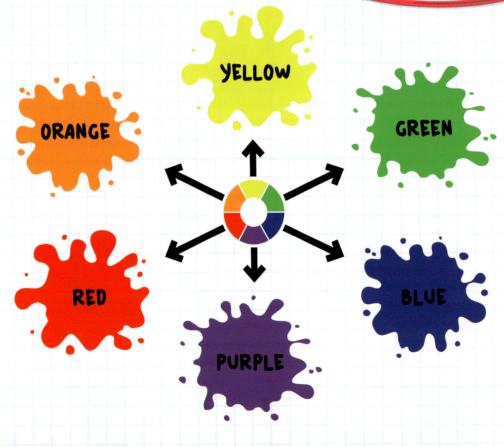

COMPLEMENTARY COLORS MAKE EACH OTHER LOOK BRIGHTER AND MORE COLORFUL.

Orange lifeboats are easy to spot against the blue water.

PASTELS AND NEONS

Adding a lot of white to your slime makes the color paler and less bright. Pale colors are called pastel colors. Use white glue and white powder to make pretty pastel slime.

PEACH SLIME

LILAC SLIME

PINK SLIME

VERY BRIGHT COLORS ARE CALLED NEON COLORS. SOME NEON COLORS EVEN GLOW IN THE DARK!

Clear glue makes neon colors look really bright!

Neon food dyes will give you really bright colors.

What happens if you mix them? Neon colors look great together!

GLOSSARY

CHEMICALS   matter that can cause changes to other matter when mixed

FINE   very thin, or made up of very small pieces

HUMAN-MADE   created by humans and not natural

LIQUID   a material that flows, such as water

MOLDABLE   can be shaped

NATURAL   found in nature and not made by people

PROPERTIES   features of something

REACTIONS   changes that happen when two or more things come into contact with each other

SENSITIVE   reacts strongly to something

SHADES   types of the same color that are darker or lighter

SOLID   firm and stable, not a liquid

INDEX

CHEMICALS 7
GLITTER 9
LIQUIDS 4, 5, 7
MATERIALS 5
NEONS 23
PASTELS 22
PREDICTIONS 14–15, 17
PRIMARY COLORS 8, 10–16, 20
PROPERTIES 5, 7
SECONDARY COLORS 12–13, 20
SOLIDS 4, 5
TREE FROGS 6